The Spirit of Islam

MUHAMMAD ASAD

THE ISLAMIC FOUNDATION

Second Edition 1980/1400 H.
Reprinted 1984.

ISBN 0 86037 050 X

THE ISLAMIC FOUNDATION
223 London Road,
Leicester, LE2 1ZE.

Qur'an House,
P.O.Box 30611
Nairobi,
Kenya.

P.M.B. 3193,
Kano,
Nigeria.

Printed by:
Henry Boot Design & Print,
Thompson Street,
Chesterfield, Derbyshire.
Telephone: 0246 208996

Foreword to the New Impression

We feel great pleasure in bringing out a new edition of this pamphlet in view of the continuing demand for short essays on various aspects of Islam. This pamphlet was originally published four years ago by the Islamic Council of Europe, being taken from a book of readings on Islam — *Islam: Its Meaning and Message,* edited by Brother Khurshid Ahmad, now Chairman of the Islamic Foundation. Its convenient size made it a specially useful addition to the growing literature on Islam, providing the busy modern reader with a succinct treatment on one particular aspect of Islam in the lucid and convincing style of an eminent author.

As the first edition ran out, and as we continued to receive enquiries and requests from various quarters, we decided to publish a second edition. Recent developments on the world stage have underlined the crucial importance of Islam in strategically vital areas. We need hardly stress the genuine need for fuller information: what matters more is that the information supplied should be both accurate and objective, presenting Islam as it really is. Nothing less can create mutual respect and understanding between Muslims and non-Muslims, as well as renewing the Muslims' own self-awareness. We believe these and similar pamphlets contribute greatly in this direction.

We pray to Allah to bless our efforts with His mercy and acceptance.

The Islamic Foundation
Leicester
18 October 1979
25 Dhu'l-Qa'da 1399

KHURRAM JAH MURAD
Director General

*The Spirit of Islam**

Muhammad Asad

ONE of the slogans most characteristic of the present age is 'the conquest of space.' Means of communication have been developed which are far beyond the dreams of former generations; and these new means have set in motion a far more rapid and extensive transfer of goods than ever before within the history of mankind. The result of this development is an economic inter-dependence of nations. No single nation or group can today afford to remain aloof from the rest of the world. Economic development has ceased to be local. Its character has become world-wide. It ignores, at least in its tendency, political boundaries and geographical distances. It carries with itself — and possibly this is even more important than the purely material side of the problem — the ever-increasing necessity of a transfer not only of merchandise but also of thoughts and cultural values. But while those two forces, the economic and the cultural, often go hand in hand, there is a difference in their dynamic rules. The elementary laws of economics require that the exchange of goods between nations be mutual; this means that no nation can act as buyer only while another nation is always seller in the long run, each of them must play both parts simultaneously, giving to, and taking from, each other, be it directly or through the medium of other actors in the play of economic forces. But in the cultural field this iron rule of exchange is not a necessity, at least not always a visible one, that is to say, the transfer of ideas and cultural influences is not necessarily based on the principle of give and take. It

* This chapter is taken from Muhammad Asad's *Islam at the Crossroads*, Lahore: Arafat Publications, 1969, pp. 7-31.

lies in human nature that nations and civilizations, which are politically and economically more virile, exert a strong fascination on the weaker or less active communities and influence them in the intellectual and social spheres without being influenced themselves.

Such is the situation today with regard to the relations between the Western and the Muslim worlds.

From the viewpoint of the historical observer the strong, one-sided influence which Western civilization at present exerts on the Muslim world is not at all surprising, because it is the outcome of a long historic process for which there are several analogies elsewhere. But while the historian may be satisfied, for us the problem remains unsettled. For us who are not mere interested spectators, but very real actors in this drama; for us who regard ourselves as the followers of Prophet Muhammad (peace and blessings be upon him) the problem in reality begins here. We believe that Islam, unlike other religions, is not only a spiritual attitude of mind, adjustable to different cultural settings, but a self-sufficing orbit of culture and a social system of clearly defined features. When, as is the case today, a foreign civilization extends its radiations into our midst and causes certain changes in our own cultural organism, we are bound to make it clear to ourselves whether that foreign influence runs in the direction of our own cultural possibilities or against them; whether it acts as an invigorating serum in the body of Islamic culture, or as a poison.

An answer to this question can be found through analysis only. We have to discover the motive forces of both civilizations — the Islamic and that of the modern West — and then to investigate how far a co-operation is possible between them. And as Islamic civilization is essentially a religious one, we must, first of all, try to define the general role of religion in human life.

Religion and Human Life

What we call the 'religious attitude' is the natural outcome of man's intellectual and biological constitution. Man is unable to explain to himself the mystery of life, the mystery of birth and death, the mystery of infinity and eternity. His reasoning stops before impregnable walls. He can, therefore, do two things only. The one is, to give up all attempts at understanding life as a totality. In this case, man will rely upon the evidence of external experiences alone and will limit his conclusions to their sphere. Thus he will be able to understand single fragments of life, which may increase in number and clarity as rapidly or as slowly as human knowledge of Nature increases, but will, nonetheless, always remain only fragments — the grasp of the totality itself remaining beyond the methodical equipment of human reason. This is the way the natural sciences go. The other possibility — which may well exist side by side with the scientific one — is the way of religion. It leads man, by means of an inner, mostly intuitive, experience, to the acceptance of a unitary explanation of life, generally on the assumption that there exists a supreme Creative Power which governs the Universe according to some pre-conceived plan above and beyond human understanding. As has just been said, this conception does not necessarily preclude man from an investigation of such facts and fragments of life as offer themselves for external observation; there is no inherent antagonism between the external (scientific) and internal (religious) perception. But the latter is, in fact, the only speculative possibility to conceive all life as a unity of essence and motive power; in short, as a well-balanced, harmonious totality. The term 'harmonious', though so terribly misused, is very important in this connection, because it implies a corresponding attitude in man himself. The religious man knows that whatever happens to him and within him can never be the result of a blind play of forces without consciousness and purpose; he believes it to be the outcome of God's conscious will alone, and, therefore, organically integrated with a universal plan. In this way man is enabled to solve the bitter antagonism between the human Self and the objective world of facts and appearances which is called Nature. The human being, with all the intricate mechanism of his soul, with all his desires and fears, his feelings and his speculative uncertainties, sees himself faced by a Nature in which bounty and cruelty, danger and security are mixed in a wondrous, inexplicable way and apparently work on lines entirely different from the methods and the structure of the human mind. Never has purely intellectual philosophy or experimental science been able to solve this conflict. This exactly is the point where religion steps in.

In the light of religious perception and experience, the human, self-conscious Self and the mute, seemingly irresponsible Nature are brought into a relation of spiritual harmony; because both, the individual consciousness of man and the Nature that surrounds him and is within him, are nothing but co-ordinate, if different, manifestations of one and the same Creative Will. The immense benefit which religion thus confers upon man is the realisation that he is, and never can cease to be, a well-planned unit in the eternal movement of Creation: a definite part in the infinite organism of universal destiny. The psychological consequence of this conception is a deep feeling of spiritual security — that balance between hopes and fears which distinguishes the positively religious man, whatever his religion, from the irreligious.

The Islamic Approach

This fundamental position is common to all great religions, whatever their specific doctrines be; and equally common to all of them is the moral appeal to man to surrender himself to the manifest Will of God. But Islam, and Islam alone, goes beyond this theoretical explanation and exhortation. It not only teaches us that all life is essentially a unity — because it proceeds from the Divine Oneness — but it shows us also the practical way how everyone of us can reproduce, within the limits of his individual, earthly life, the unity of Idea and Action both in his existence and in his consciousness. To attain that supreme goal of life, man is, in Islam, not compelled to renounce the world; no austerities are required to open a secret door to spiritual purification; no pressure is exerted upon the mind to believe incomprehensible dogmas in order that salvation be secured. Such things are utterly foreign to Islam: for it is neither a mystical doctrine nor a philosophy. It is simply a programme of life according to the rules of Nature which God has decreed upon His creation; and its supreme achievement is the complete co-ordination of the spiritual and the material aspects of human life. In the teachings of Islam, both these aspects are not only 'reconciled' to each other in the sense of leaving no inherent conflict between the bodily and the moral existence of man, but the fact of their co-existence and actual inseparability is insisted upon as the natural basis of life.

This, I think, is the reason for the peculiar form of the Islamic prayer in which spiritual concentration and certain bodily movements are co-ordinated with each other. Inimical critics of Islam often select this way of praying as a proof of their allegation that Islam is a religion of formalism and outwardness. And, in fact, people of other religions, who are accustomed to neatly separate the 'spiritual' from the 'bodily' almost in the same way as the dairyman separates the cream from the milk, cannot easily understand that in the unskimmed milk of Islam both these ingredients, though distinct in their respective constitutions, harmoniously live and express themselves together. In other words, the Islamic prayer consists of mental concentration and bodily movements because human life itself is of such a composition, and because we are supposed to approach God through the sum-total of all the faculties He has bestowed upon us.

A further illustration of this attitude can be seen in the institution of the *ṭawāf,* the ceremony of walking round the *Ka'bah* in Makka.[1] As it is an indispensable obligation for everyone who enters the Holy City to go seven times round the *Ka'bah,* and as the observance of this injunction is one of the three most essential points of the pilgrimage, we have the right to ask ourselves: What is the meaning of this? Is it necessary to express devotion in such a formal way?

The answer is quite obvious. If we move in a circle around some object we thereby establish that object as the central point of our action. The *Ka'bah,* towards which every Muslim turns his face in prayer, symbolises the Oneness of God. The bodily movement of the pilgrims in the *ṭawāf* symbolises the activity of human life. Consequently, the *ṭawāf* implies that not only our devotional thoughts but also our practical life, our actions and endeavours, must have the idea of God and His Oneness for their centre — in accordance with the words of the Holy Qur'ān:

> 'I have not created Jinn and Man but that they should worship Me' (al-Qur'ān, 51: 56).

Thus, the conception of 'worship' in Islam is different from that in any other religion. Here it is not restricted to the purely devotional practices, for example, prayers or fasting, but extends over the whole of man's practical life as well. If the object of our life as a whole is to be the worship of God, we necessarily must regard this life, in the totality of all its aspects, as one complex moral responsibility. Thus, all our actions even the seemingly trivial ones, must be performed as acts of worship; that is, performed consciously as constituting a part of God's universal plan. Such a state of things is, for the man of average capability, a distant ideal; but is it not the purpose of religion to bring ideals into real existence?

The position of Islam in this respect is unmistakable. It teaches us, firstly, that the permanent worship of God in all the manifold actions of human life is the very meaning of this life; and, secondly, that the achievement of this purpose remains impossible so long as we divide our life into two parts, the spiritual and the material: they must be bound together, in our consciousness and our action, into one harmo-

1. Makka is usually written as Mecca. In this book, the word has been spelled uniformly as Makka.—Editor.

nious entity. Our notion of God's Oneness must be reflected in our own striving towards a co-ordination and unification of the various aspects of our life.

A logical consequence of this attitude is a further difference between Islam and all other known religious systems. It is to be found in the fact that Islam, as a teaching, undertakes to define not only the metaphysical relations between man and his Creator but also — and with scarcely less insistence — the earthly relations between the individual and his social surroundings. The worldly life is not regarded as a mere empty shell, as a meaningless shadow of the Hereafter that is to come, but as a self-contained, positive entity. God Himself is a Unity not only in essence but also in purpose; and therefore, His creation is a Unity, possibly in essence, but certainly in purpose.

Perfection: The Islamic Ideal

Worship of God in the wide sense just explained constitutes, according to Islam, the meaning of human life. And it is this conception alone that shows us the possibility of man's reaching perfection within his individual, earthly life. Of all religious systems, Islam alone declares that individual perfection is possible in our earthly existence. Islam does not postpone this fulfilment until after a suppression of the so-called 'bodily' desires, as the Christian teaching does; nor does Islam promise a continuous chain of rebirths on a progressively higher plane, as is the case with Hinduism; nor does Islam agree with Buddhism, according to which perfection and salvation can only be obtained through an annihilation of the individual Self and its emotional links with the world. NO: Islam is emphatic in the assertion that man can reach perfection in the earthly, individual life and by making full use of all the worldly possibilities of his life.

To avoid misunderstandings, the term 'perfection' will have to be defined in the sense it is used here. As long as we have to do with human, biologically limited beings, we cannot possibly consider the idea of 'absolute' perfection, because everything absolute belongs to the realm of Divine attributes alone. Human perfection, in its true psychological and moral sense, must necessarily have a relative and purely individual bearing. It does not imply the possession of all imaginable good qualities, nor even the progressive acquisition of new qualities from outside, but solely the development of the already existing, positive qualities of the individual in such a way as to rouse his innate but otherwise dormant powers. Owing to the natural variety of the life-phenomena, the inborn qualities of man differ in each individual case. It would be absurd, therefore, to suppose that all human beings should, or even could, strive towards one and the same 'type' of perfection — just as it would be absurd to expect a perfect race-horse and a perfect heavy draught horse to possess exactly the same qualities. Both may be individually perfect and satisfactory, but they will be different, because their original characters are different. With human beings the case is similar. If perfection were to be standardised in a certain 'type' — as Christianity does in the type of the ascetic saint — men would have to give up, or change, or suppress, their individual differentiation. But this would clearly violate the divine law of individual variety which dominates all life on this earth. Therefore Islam, which is not a religion of repression, allows to man a very wide margin in his personal and social existence, so that the various qualities, temperaments and psychological inclinations of different individuals should find their way to positive development according to their individual predisposition. Thus a man may be an ascetic, or he may enjoy the full measure of his sensual possibilities within the lawful limits; he may be a nomad roaming through the deserts, without food for tomorrow, or a rich merchant surrounded by his goods. As long as he sincerely and consciously submits to the laws decreed by God, he is free to shape his personal life to whatever form his nature directs him. His duty is to make the best of himself so that he might honour the life-gift which His Creator has bestowed upon him; and to help his fellow-beings, by means of his own development, in their spiritual, social and material endeavours. But the form of his individual life is in no way fixed by a standard. He is free to make his choice from among all the limitless lawful possibilities open to him.

The basis of this 'liberalism' in Islam, is to be found in the conception that man's original nature is essentially good. Contrary to the Christian idea that man is born sinful, or the teachings of Hinduism, that he is originally low and impure and must painfully stagger through a long chain of transmigrations towards the ultimate goal of Perfection, the Islamic teaching contends that man is born pure and — in the sense explained above — potentially perfect. It is said in the Holy Qur'ān:

'Surely We created man in the best structure.'

But in the same breath the verse continues:

'... and afterwards We reduced him to the lowest of low: with the exception of those who have faith and do good works.' (al-Qur'ān, 95: 4, 5).

In this verse is expressed the doctrine that man is originally good and pure; and, furthermore, that disbelief in God and lack of good actions may destroy his original perfection. On the other hand, man may retain, or regain, that original, individual perfection if he consciously realises God's Oneness and submits to His laws. Thus, according to Islam, evil is never essential or even original; it is an acquisition of man's later life, and is due to a misuse of the innate, positive qualities with which God has endowed every human being. Those qualities are, as has been said before, different in every individual, but always potentially perfect in themselves; and their full development is possible within the period of man's individual life on earth. We take it for granted that the life after death, owing to its entirely changed conditions of feeling and perception, will confer upon us other, quite new, qualities and faculties which will make a still further progress of the human soul possible; but this concerns our future life alone. In this earthly life also, the Islamic teaching definitely asserts, we—every-one of us — can reach a full measure of perfection by developing the positive, already existing traits of which our individualities are composed.

Of all religions, Islam alone makes it possible for man to enjoy the full range of his earthly life without for a moment losing its spiritual orientation. How entirely different is this from the Christian conception! According to the Christian dogma, mankind stumbles under a hereditary sin committed by Adam and Eve, and consequently the whole life is looked upon — in dogmatic theory at least — as a gloomy vale of sorrows. It is the battlefield of two opposing forces: the evil, represented by Satan, and the good, represented by Jesus Christ. Satan tries, by means of bodily temptations, to bar the progress of the human soul towards the light eternal; the soul belongs to Christ, while the body is the playground of satanic influences. One could express it differently: the world of Matter is essentially satanic, while the world of Spirit is divine and good. Everything in human nature that is material, or 'carnal', as Christian theology prefers to call it, is a direct result of Adam's succumbing to the advice of the hellish Prince of Darkness and Matter. Therefore, to obtain salvation, man must turn his heart away from this world of the flesh towards the future, spiritual world, where the 'sin of mankind' is redeemed by the sacrifice of Christ on the cross.

Even if this dogma is not — and never was — obeyed in practice, the very existence of such a teaching tends to produce a permanent feeling of bad conscience in the religiously inclined man. He is tossed about between the peremptory call to neglect the world and the natural urge of his heart to live and to enjoy this life. The very idea of an unavoidable, because inherited, sin, and of its mystical — to the average intellect incomprehensible — redemption through the suffering of Jesus on the cross, erects a barrier between man's spiritual longing and his legitimate desire to live.

In Islam, we know nothing of Original Sin; we regard it as incongruent with the idea of God's justice; God does not make the child responsible for the doings of his father: and how could He have made all those numberless generations of mankind responsible for a sin of disobedience committed by a remote ancestor? It is no doubt possible to construct philosophical explanations of this strange assumption, but for the unsophisticated intellect it will always remain as artificial and as unsatisfactory as the conception of Trinity itself. And as there is no hereditary sin, there is also no universal redemption of mankind in the teachings of Islam. Redemption and damnation are individual. Every Muslim is his own redeemer; he bears all possibilities of spiritual success and failure within his heart. It is said in the Qur'ān of the human personality:

> 'In its favour is that which it has earned and against it is that which it has become guilty of.' (al-Qur'ān, 2: 286).

Another verse says:

> 'Nothing shall be reckoned to man but that which he has striven for.' (al-Qur'ān, 53: 39).

The Middle Way

But if Islam does not share the gloomy aspect of life as expressed in Christianity, it teaches us, nonetheless, not to attribute to earthly life that exaggerated value which modern Western civilisation attributes to it. While the Christian outlook implies that earthly life is a bad business, the modern West — as distinct from Christianity — adores life in exactly the same way as the glutton adores his food: he devours it, but has no respect for it. Islam on the other hand, looks upon earthly life with calm and respect. It does not worship it, but regards it as an organic stage on our way to a higher existence. But just because it is a stage and a necessary stage, too, man has no right to despise or even to underrate the value of his earthly life. Our travel through this world is a necessary positive part in God's plan. Human life, therefore, is of tremendous value; but we must never forget that it is a purely instrumental value. In Islam there is no room for the materialistic optimism of of the modern West which says: 'My Kingdom is of this world alone.' — nor for the life-contempt of the Christian saying: 'My Kingdom is not of this world.' Islam goes the middle way. The Qur'ān teaches us to pray:

> 'Our Lord, give us the good in this world and the good in the Hereafter.' (al-Qur'ān, 2: 201).

Thus, the full appreciation of this world and its goods is in no way a handicap for our spiritual endeavours. Material prosperity is desirable, though not a goal in itself. The goal of all our practical activities always ought to be the creation and the maintenance of such personal and social conditions as might be helpful for the development of moral stamina in men. In accordance with this principle, Islam leads man towards a consciousness of moral responsibility in everything he does, whether great or small. The well-known injunction of the Gospels: 'Give Caesar that which belongs to Caesar, and give God that which belongs to God' — has no room in the theological structure of Islam, because Islam does not admit the existence of a conflict between the moral and the socio-economic requirements of our existence. In everything there can be only one choice: the choice between Right and Wrong — and nothing in-between. Hence the intense insistence on action as an indispensable element of morality.

Every individual Muslim has to regard himself as personally responsible for all happenings around him, and to strive for the establishment of Right and the abolition of Wrong at every time and in every direction. A sanction for this attitude is to be found in the verse of the Qur'ān:

> 'You are the best community that has been sent forth to mankind: You enjoin the Right and forbid the Wrong; and you have faith in God.' (al-Qur'ān, 3: 110).

This is the moral justification of the healthy activism of Islam, a justification of the early Islamic conquests. It has meant, as it means today, the construction of a worldly frame for the best possible spiritual development of man. For, according to the teachings of Islam, moral knowledge automatically forces moral responsibility upon man. A mere Platonic discernment between Right and Wrong, without the urge to promote Right and to destroy Wrong, is a gross immorality in itself. In Islam, morality lives and dies with the human endeavour to establish its victory upon earth.

طبع بتصريح وزارة الاعلام

رقم ٥٨٥٨ م ج

بتاريخ ٨ /٩/ ١٤١١ هـ

SAHAR PRINTING PRESS